Contents

No place like home?

We all need shelter of some kind. Shelter protects us from the elements, keeps us warm (or cool), and gives us a feeling of security. But most of us need more than that. We don't just want to feel safe or warm, we want to belong and to feel part of a community. We want somewhere we can call home.

The impact of homes

Our homes affect us, but they also affect our surroundings, or environment, both directly and indirectly. How they look, how and where they are built, all have an impact on our surroundings. But they have a much wider impact, too. At home we consume huge quantities of resources, such as energy and water. These are the things we use as part of our everyday lives. Obtaining and using those resources can be highly damaging to the environment. Nearly a third of total energy used in most European countries goes into homes. In the USA the figure is about 20 per cent. In many developing countries, the proportion is far higher, although they use much less energy overall. This is because they depend more on agriculture than industry. In India, for example, 91 per cent of all energy used in the country goes into homes. As these developing countries become more industrialised, however, this is likely to change.

This dome eco-house has been built using recycled or natural materials, such as wood, that have come from a sustainable source. Energy is supplied by solar panels and a wind turbine. The dome shape reduces heat loss and the use of building materials by 30 per cent.

Our daily activities are also responsible for producing large amounts of waste. Some of it takes years, even centuries, to break down. Some of these wastes are toxic, particularly when burned. Others can be harmful for different reasons. Many of the chemicals we use in the home are toxic and may have long-term damaging effects, both for people and the environment.

A sustainable home?

We all want to feel comfortable and secure in our homes. But that doesn't have to create a massive impact on the environment. We can make our homes great places to live without 'costing the Earth'. Perhaps more importantly, doing this may mean our children, and their children, can do the same. This is what is meant by sustainable living.

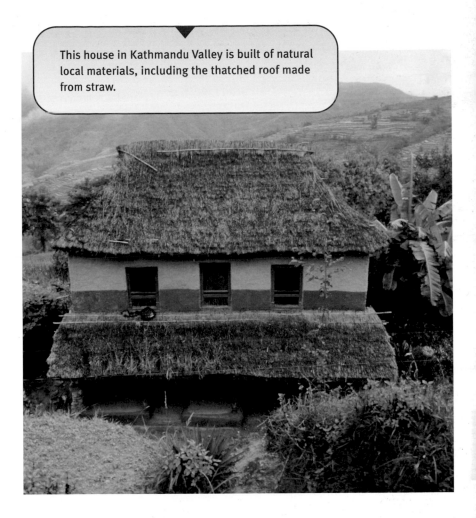

This house in Kathmandu Valley is built of natural local materials, including the thatched roof made from straw.

Different lives – different sustainable homes

David lives on a housing estate in the UK. From the outside the houses look normal, but when you look closer you can see that parts of the roof are covered with dark panels. These are solar heaters that use the energy of the Sun to heat water. Inside you become aware of a slight hum. This is a low-speed fan, drawing in air through the roof, improving ventilation and reducing moisture. As you look around, you notice the light bulbs look strange. The more you look the more you can see that this is not an ordinary house at all. It is a sustainable home.

Kerry's house doesn't look normal, even from the outside. It juts out, like a huge, steel-clad wedge from granite boulders, overlooking a bay in Nova Scotia. At the centre of the living space is a sky-lit courtyard that helps control

conditions within the house: creating its own microclimate. Windows on the east side of the house are larger than on the west and allow in more light and less heat in the summer. Much of the structure is made from local materials and the design matches the rugged landscape into which it is built. It is also a sustainable home.

Vaneeta's home is near Durban in Kwa-Zulu Natal Province, South Africa. Hers is one of over 6000 homes built by the residents themselves under a national government scheme. Mud bricks conserve heat at night and keep rooms cool during the day. The project also uses natural features, making use of local plants and the natural slopes and drainage to filter water. Vaneeta lives in a sustainable home, too.

5

Sustainable development

Living sustainably means providing for our needs without damaging the environment, or the ability of others to meet their own needs, both now and in the future. Applying this to all aspects of how we live, including our homes, is known as sustainable development.

Quality of life

The idea of sustainable development goes much further than using resources wisely or protecting our surroundings. It is also about the way we live, which is sometimes called 'quality of life'. There is a close link between the quality of people's homes and their quality of life. For example, poor quality or inadequate housing is often linked to a lack of resources or facilities in the area. This may in turn be linked to poverty, unemployment and even poor health. Sustainable housing can reverse this process by linking good quality housing to work and training opportunities and good local services (such as shops, schools and transport). The homes themselves, in the way they are built and operate, can help create healthy living conditions. In this way people's health and well-being starts to be linked to the health and well-being of the environment.

A poor Haitian couple stands with their child in the doorway of a rundown shack that is their home. Poor quality homes like this contribute to other problems, such as poor health.

There are several schemes around the world involved with building eco-homes. These volunteers in Wales are building a straw bale house using natural materials as part of a project set up by the Centre for Alternative Technology.

Eco-homes

'EcoHomes' is an example of a scheme that gives some idea of what is involved in the idea of sustainable homes. This UK scheme rates homes on their sustainability. It balances environmental issues such as resource use and impact on wildlife, against the need for affordable, high quality, safe and healthy homes. Homes are judged on:

- energy
- public transport links
- pollution
- use of materials
- water use
- land use
- ecology
- the health and well-being of the inhabitants.

Each of these areas has a score attached to it. The scores combine to form a rating and the aim is to achieve a 'good' or better rating for all new and refurbished homes from 2005 onwards.

Case Study: Tlholego eco-village

The Tlholego eco-village is situated on 1.5 square kilometres in the north-west province of South Africa. It was established in 1991 in order to provide a rural 'living and learning centre' involving poor workers and unemployed city-dwellers. Homes are owner-built using low cost methods and building materials, such as ferro-cement, that do little damage to the environment. Ferro-cement is strong, but light, and uses smaller amounts of cement than normal concrete. This avoids the poor quality and environmental problems of normal, low-cost housing. Tlholego also trains people in the design and set-up of sustainable village communities, including a farm school for 250 students from the surrounding community. In 2000, the village was chosen by the National Department of Housing as a 'model representing South Africa's solutions towards sustainable development'.

Different places, different homes

Different environments require different measures to achieve sustainability. For example, in much of northern Europe and North America, the need to keep homes warm during a large part of the year means that energy-saving measures are of major importance. In warmer climates, keeping cool is usually of more importance.

Fitting in

Sustainable homes should also make use of local building materials and fit in with the local landscape. The location of a sustainable home will determine the choice of materials used, such as timber, stone or earth, according to what is available locally.

Home grown

In Mali, Guinea, many of the houses have thatched roofs that match the slope of the landscape. The eastern side of these houses is constructed of woven bamboo. The remaining walls are built of stabilised, rammed, or compressed, earth, rather than 'fired' bricks. Brick kilns, needed to harden normal bricks, are banned in Mali because they burn wood, which leads to deforestation. Making rammed earth bricks, using a hand-operated press, is an ancient skill in Guinea. Now the technology has been adapted by stabilising the soil with small amounts of cement to make the bricks stronger. Roof tiles are made in the same way, but fibre from locally grown plants, rather than cement, is used to stabilise the tiles.

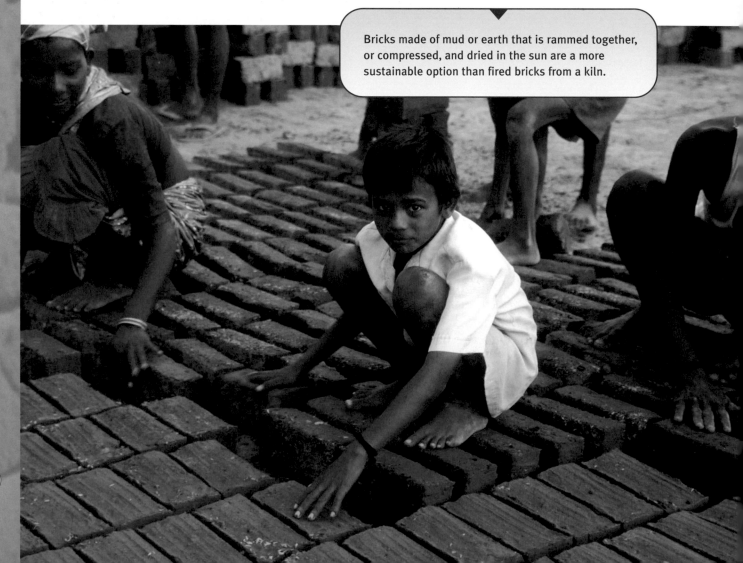

Bricks made of mud or earth that is rammed together, or compressed, and dried in the sun are a more sustainable option than fired bricks from a kiln.

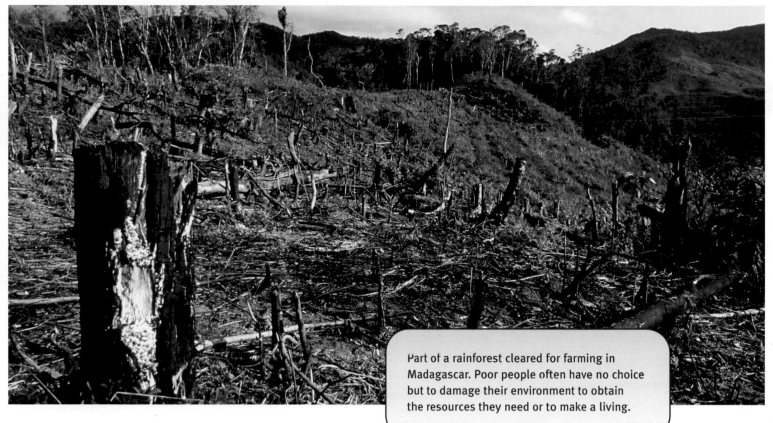

Part of a rainforest cleared for farming in Madagascar. Poor people often have no choice but to damage their environment to obtain the resources they need or to make a living.

Rich and poor

In the developing world, such as parts of Africa and Asia, people often have no choice but to live unsustainably. They may be forced to damage their environment, by clearing forests for example, in order to survive. Much of the deforestation in these areas, however, is caused by developers clearing land to grow crops or graze cattle. In the developed countries of Europe and North America, most people live unsustainably in a different way, by consuming too many resources and creating pollution. The idea of sustainable homes will therefore have different meanings in these different situations.

There are also differences between rural and urban communities. In developing countries, many people move from rural areas into cities to look for work. This often puts enormous pressure on urban resources such as energy and clean water. Developing more sustainable ways of rural living can encourage people to stay in rural areas and slow the movement into cities. This may be through developing better agricultural methods or using natural forest products such as fruits, nuts, natural cosmetics and medicines as a source of income. Where the technology, such as

Internet access, is available small businesses or service industries can also do well. By relieving the pressure on urban resources and making rural living more sustainable both areas are more environmentally friendly.

In developed and some developing countries more people live in towns and cities, and those that don't often commute to urban areas to work. This could change. As more people in rural areas begin to use their homes as workplaces, via computers with Internet access, or set up their own local businesses, the pressure on city environments is reduced. This may result in less reliance on cars and other services, reducing the impact on resources such as fuel.

Footprints on the Earth

We live in a world where enormous inequalities and differences exist. Even with these inequalities, we are still using far more resources than the Earth can sustain. No matter where we live, sustainable homes should be about reducing our own impact, or footprint, on the Earth, while allowing others a fairer share.

The energy-saving home

We need energy to live and work. Only when energy is converted from one form to another, for example, from the chemical energy in oil to the heat energy in a boiler, can work take place. When an energy conversion takes place, some energy is always wasted. This is important in understanding ideas about the energy-saving home.

We live in an energy-hungry world that relies heavily on fossil fuels (coal, oil and gas). We may have another 40 years of oil left in the ground and 60 years of gas if we go on using them at the present rate. Coal will last a lot longer, but its use is more damaging to the environment. We know that burning any fossil fuel produces waste gases that are harmful to the environment. The most significant of these is carbon dioxide, which is a greenhouse gas. Greenhouse gases cause warming of the Earth's atmosphere by absorbing energy that radiates from the Earth's surface. Although this is a natural process, increases in carbon dioxide levels in the last 100 years have produced an additional warming effect. Many people believe this is now affecting our global climate and causing sea levels to rise.

The energy trap

There is another problem, too. Many people simply cannot afford, or obtain, the fuel they need to keep warm or cook their food. Even in the richer parts of the world, people can become ill or die of cold (or dampness) due to lack of heating. In poorer regions, people may be forced to clear forests and woodland in search of firewood to cook with. Alternatively, they may have to burn animal dung, which means wasting a valuable fertiliser. All these people are trapped in what is called 'energy poverty'.

An adult and child carry firewood home in Guatemala, Central America. As forests are cleared, people have to travel further to find fuel. This means less time is available for work, or for children to go to school.

Finding the right fuel for the job

In the developed world most household energy is used to heat water or the home itself (space heating), often by electricity. Electricity is an expensive and wasteful way of heating air or water, because there are already large energy losses during its generation in power stations. Heating directly by oil is better because there are fewer energy conversions. Gas heating, using what are known as condensing boilers, is more energy efficient still (and less polluting), as long as gas is available.

Combined heat and power

Combined heat and power (CHP), also known as cogeneration, is an efficient technology in which the heat produced during the generation of electricity is recovered and used for industrial purposes, public buildings, leisure complexes and community heating. CHP can achieve a 35 per cent reduction in energy use compared with power stations and heat-only boilers. Micro-CHP involves a small generator, about the size of a normal boiler, which provides heat and power to a single home or small residential block.

A dragline used to obtain coal from an open cast mine in Australia. Many countries rely heavily on coal to meet their energy needs. Coal produces more polluting gases than either oil or natural gas, although all of these fossil fuels produce carbon dioxide when they burn.

space heating 58%

water heating 24%

lights and appliances 13%

cooking 5%

This pie chart shows a breakdown of energy use in a typical home in north-west Europe. In many poorer, developing countries most domestic energy is used for cooking.

Source: Renewable Energy: Power for a Sustainable Future, OUP 2004.

Biomass fuels

An important source of energy, particularly in developing countries, is biomass. Biomass fuels are solid, liquid or gas fuels produced from animal or plant material such as agricultural waste or dung. Solid biomass fuels, such as straw and wood, may be burned to generate electricity or to provide heating directly, often as part of a local CHP scheme. Unlike fossil fuels, biomass fuels can be described as 'carbon neutral'. This means the carbon dioxide produced when the fuel burns is balanced by the carbon dioxide that was absorbed by the plant material when it was growing. In theory, therefore, it does not contribute to global warming as there is no overall addition to carbon dioxide levels. This is only true, of course, if the fuel is replaced at the same rate as it is used up. In the case of wood this often does not happen because trees are not always replanted. In fact, the widespread use of firewood in many regions of the world, particularly Africa and Asia, is a major cause of deforestation as trees are cut down for heating and cooking purposes.

Most biomass fuels can also be described as renewable because there is a continuous supply of the raw materials needed to make the fuel. Again however, this only applies to wood if new trees are planted to replace those used.

Biogas

Gas biomass fuels, or biogas, are produced by fermenting specially grown crops (such as sugar cane or maize) or animal, human or plant waste. In poor or isolated communities, small biogas fermenters use straw and other waste material to produce a continuous supply of gas fuel. In India there are nearly 4 million small biogas units, but they are unsuitable for urban environments for reasons of space and safety. Larger, community biogas plants can be more efficient, but it is sometimes difficult to balance ownership of the materials used (such as animal dung) and the amount of biogas made available to each member of the community.

This biogas fermenter in Bandarawella, Sri Lanka, has been supplying most of the energy needs of this family's home since 2000. Biogas production involves chanelling cow manure to a closed storage tank where it breaks down and releases methane. The gas is then piped into the home to use as fuel.

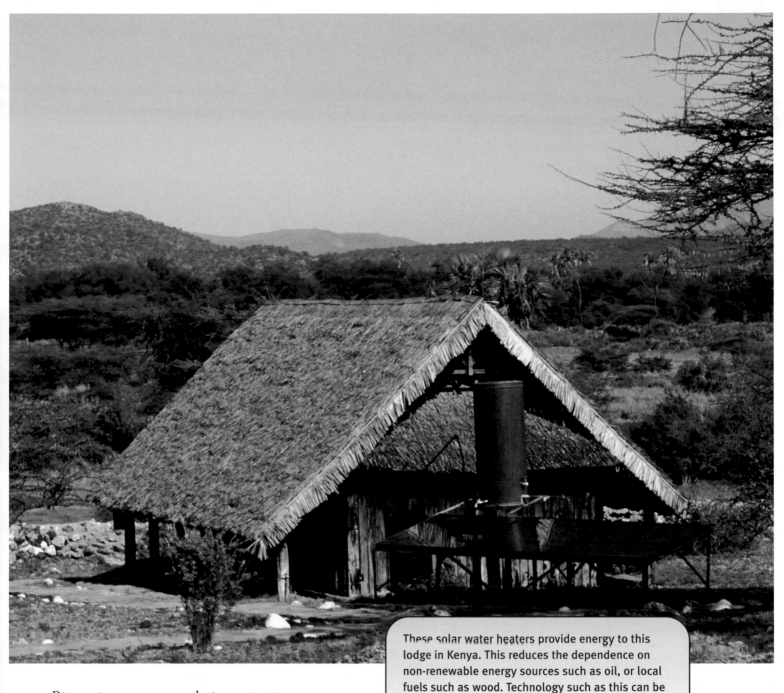

These solar water heaters provide energy to this lodge in Kenya. This reduces the dependence on non-renewable energy sources such as oil, or local fuels such as wood. Technology such as this can be used to provide energy for homes, making them more sustainable.

Biogas is an enormously important energy source in the search for more sustainable homes. Its use in poorer regions such as Africa and India can reduce dependence on wood, which in turn decreases pressure on forests. Similarly, it can reduce the need for fossil fuels, which may be too expensive or unavailable, anyway. In addition, the remaining slurry inside the fermenters forms a valuable fertiliser for crops.

Doing it the renewable way

There are many other sources of renewable energy, most notably the Sun and wind. Solar water heaters, usually mounted on roofs, use the Sun's rays to heat water that is circulating in copper pipes on black, insulated plates. Solar heaters work in both direct sunlight and overcast conditions and can provide 50–70 per cent of a typical European household's hot water during the year. Kenya is the global leader in solar power systems per person. More than 30,000 are sold annually, mainly for water heating. It is estimated that with better marketing and support for solar energy over 400,000 square metres of solar panels could be installed. This would reduce Kenya's annual oil imports by 4 per cent, with a saving of around £17 million.

Electricity from the Sun

Sunlight can generate electricity directly or charge up batteries using photovoltaic (PV) cells. A typical household PV array can generate around 1–3 kilowatts. In a developed country, that's about a third of an average family's electricity demand. In poorer countries, such as India, photovoltaic cells are widely used to power lanterns, street lighting and market stalls, and for pumping water for drinking and irrigation. Because they are quite portable, they have even been used to provide power for lanterns in a Tibetan nomad's tent!

Case Study: Solar energy in the Auroville township

The Auroville township in India uses a variety of solar technologies to heat both water and food. Small, solar box cookers heat food using sunlight reflected from an angled mirror. Their use reduces reliance on bottled gas, which is expensive and contributes to global warming. Larger designs are more efficient, however.

This giant solar dish provides power for the Auroville township by harnessing the Sun's energy.

In Auroville, a 15-metre-diameter curved dish, built of thousands of small mirrors, concentrates enough of the Sun's energy to heat water to cook 2000 meals a day!

Buildings also make use of what is known as passive solar design. Natural lighting and good ventilation, shading of walls and good insulation of roofs create cool, 'comfort zones' within buildings during the heat of the day.

Domestic wind turbines supply electricity to this Danish community. Wind power is a renewable, non-polluting energy source, although noise and so-called visual pollution can be a disadvantage.

Passive solar design

Trapping the Sun's energy does not necessarily need special equipment. Passive solar design involves the careful planning of buildings so they make maximum use of the Sun's energy. This can be achieved by building 'solar stores'. These are spaces within the building, with glass exteriors, that work in a similar way to greenhouses. Installing the largest windows in the best-lit (south facing in the northern hemisphere and north facing in the southern hemisphere) walls has a similar effect.

In addition, houses can be built of materials, such as concrete, stone and earth, with high 'thermal mass'. This means they heat up slowly in the day, but then retain the heat and allow it to escape slowly back into the house at night. In Tlholego eco-village, in rural South Africa, this type of passive solar technology saves residents up to 50 or 60 per cent in energy costs.

Wind power

Although large, commercial wind turbines are used throughout the world to generate electricity, smaller, community-based turbines are also an important source of locally- generated energy. This is especially true in poor or isolated communities. Like solar energy, wind-generated power does not produce greenhouse gases. Small wind turbines also avoid some of the disadvantages, such as noise, land use and 'visual pollution', of the larger turbines used in wind farms. Small turbines are, however, less efficient. In Denmark 75 per cent of wind turbines are owned by local co-operatives. In India simple wind turbines raise water from tube wells. These are wells that are drilled to reach water deep under ground. Pumps are therefore needed to raise the water to the surface. Wind turbines are as effective as diesel-powered pumps, but do less damage to the environment and do not rely on a supply of oil.

Moving air

Good ventilation helps control temperatures by regulating the flow of air and reducing draughts. This, in turn, reduces the amount of energy needed for heating or air conditioning. It also cuts down dampness due to condensation caused by moist, warm air meeting colder air. In positive pressure ventilation, a slow-speed fan in the ceiling draws in air from outside through the roof. This pushes out moisture-laden air and replaces it with fresher, drier air.

Cutting down on energy

Most modern electrical and gas appliances are far more energy-efficient than in the past. Many now have some form of energy efficiency logo or badge. In the European Union this is a rating from A (the most efficient) to G. In Asia and the Pacific (for example, Japan, Indonesia and the Philippines) about three-quarters of countries have some form of energy-efficiency labelling. In the USA most shops and suppliers display an Energy Guide allowing buyers to compare the energy-efficiency of all appliances on sale. In other countries, particularly in the southern hemisphere, appliances such as refrigerators have been developed that are powered by biogas or by photovoltaic cells that use energy from the Sun.

Nothing new

Passive ventilation in homes makes use of simple design features and involves no moving parts at all. Vertical ducts or pipes run from the kitchen and bathroom to vents (openings) in the roof, drawing moist air out of the building. Traditional methods of passive ventilation have been used in desert countries for thousands of years. These make use of the large variations in temperature between day and night and in different parts of the building. They depend on air being drawn from cooler parts of the building as warmer air is allowed to escape.

These homes in Croydon, UK, are part of an eco-friendly housing estate. These homes make use of passive ventilation through the ducts on top of the roofs.

Although more expensive, energy-efficient light bulbs (compact fluorescent lights, or CFLs) can save up to ten times the cost of operating an ordinary bulb over its lifetime as well as saving electricity. Because of their low energy requirements, CFLs are also ideal for using with photovoltaic cells. Further savings can be achieved with automatic light sensors in communal areas, such as inside passages or courtyards in flats, which mean lights are not left on needlessly.

Insulating walls, by filling wall cavities (the space between the inner and outer wall) with various types of insulating material, can reduce heat loss by over 40 per cent. Loft insulation can reduce heat loss by 20 per cent, while carpets can reduce heat loss through floors by 60 per cent. Some types of insulating material can be responsible for generating toxic by-products, however, both during their manufacture and use. Double or triple glazing will cut down heat loss through windows, but can be expensive. Like some forms of insulation, manufacturing the frames – usually from material called uPVC – can also produce harmful by-products.

What colour is your electricity?

In many countries, it is now possible to switch the electricity supply to one known as 'green power'. This means the supplier has to match the energy used with electricity produced from a renewable source, such as wind or biomass. In the USA, more than 50 per cent of households have an option to purchase some form of green power although not all do. All US consumers can also purchase 'renewable energy certificates'. This means some of the money from their energy bills supports sustainable energy projects elsewhere in the world.

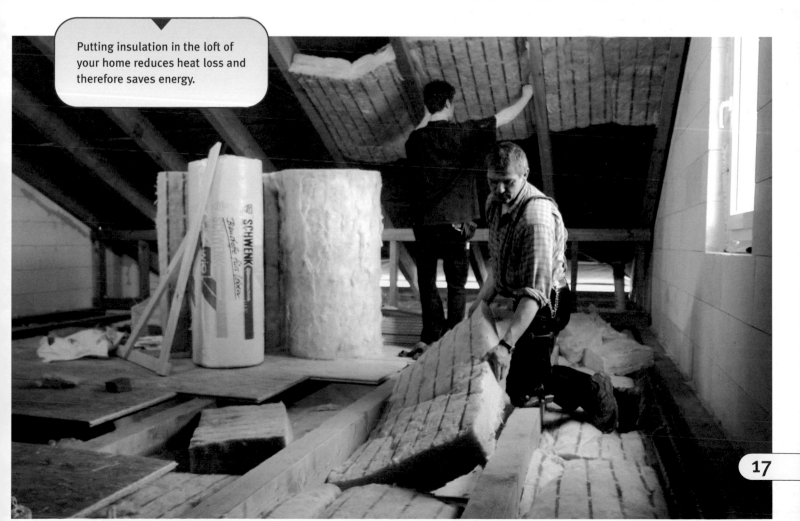

Putting insulation in the loft of your home reduces heat loss and therefore saves energy.

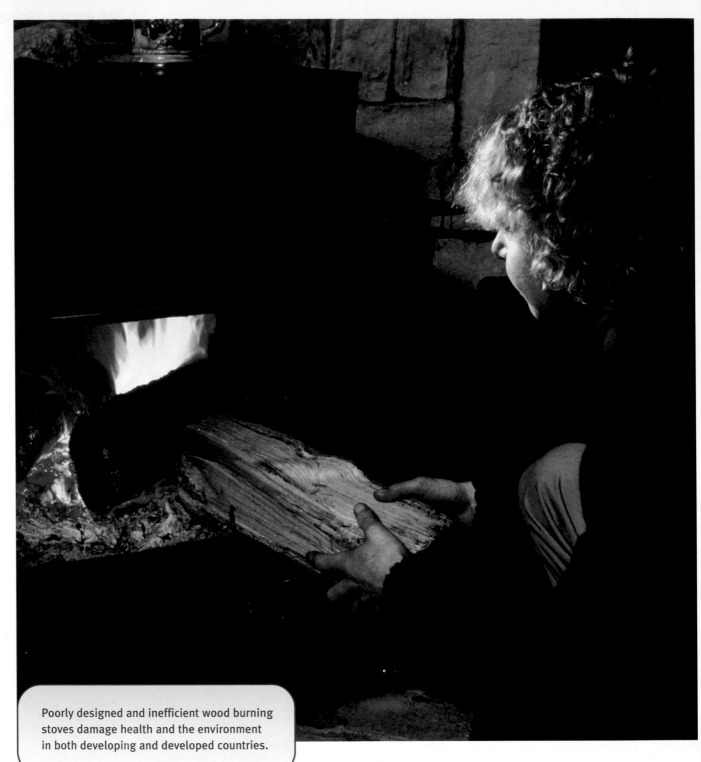

Poorly designed and inefficient wood burning stoves damage health and the environment in both developing and developed countries.

Energy kills?

Perhaps surprisingly, one of the biggest killers in many developing countries is the wood-burning stove. The inefficient way these stoves burn produces smoke particles that enter and damage the lungs. Poisonous gases, such as carbon monoxide, and cancer-causing chemicals, such as dioxins, are also produced. Worldwide, up to 2 billion people may be exposed to higher risks of lung disease in this way.

Damage to health caused by burning wood is not only an issue for poor countries. It is estimated there are 11 million wood-burning stoves, used for cooking and heating, in the USA, burning 43 million tons of wood each year. Burning a kilogram of wood, even in a modern wood stove, releases into the atmosphere 130 grams of carbon monoxide and 10 grams of carcinogenic (cancer-causing) benzene. A typical US wood-burning stove is several thousand times 'dirtier' than burning natural gas, for the same amount of energy released.

Case Study: Making a better stove

Energy-efficient stoves are designed so that the wood or animal dung burns at a higher temperature, and so fewer toxic products are produced. They also burn less fuel so less wood is used. In the case of dung this means that more can be left available to use as fertiliser rather than fuel. There are many other ways of increasing the efficiency of stoves, such as adding a chimney to increase the flow of air over the fire. A 'pot skirt' that channels hot air against the bottom and sides of the pot also helps to increase efficiency. Even more effective, however, is to have part of the pot set into the stove itself. Recent cooking stove designs in India encourage the use of family cooking pots as a template when constructing new stoves. This means the pot fits snugly against the heat source.

This twin-pot wood burning stove uses fuel more efficiently than traditional stoves. It allows one pot to heat rapidly, while the other is left simmering.

Living with less water

You might not think so, but water is a scarce resource. Most parts of the world experience water shortages at some time during the year. As the global climate changes and becomes more unpredictable, the availability of water is likely to become an increasingly pressing problem for most homes, wherever they are.

Water use

This is not just a question of water availability. Supplying homes with water and, just as importantly, treating the dirty water we produce uses energy – about 220 kilowatt-hours for an average European household every year. That's enough to boil a kettle for 100 hours!

In the developed world, we are using more and more water in our homes. In the UK, for example, water consumption has risen by over 70 per cent in the last 30 years. North America's largest aquifer (underground water supply), the Ogallala, is being used up at the rate of 12 billion cubic metres a year. Agriculture and increasing demand from cities accounts for much of this. In developing parts of the world, increasing water use is also a problem. In cities, increasing numbers of better-off families are demanding better standards of living, including improved water supplies. In rural areas, growing cash crops, such as coffee, for export to richer countries puts still more pressure on scarce groundwater supplies. Often these crops require more water than traditional varieties.

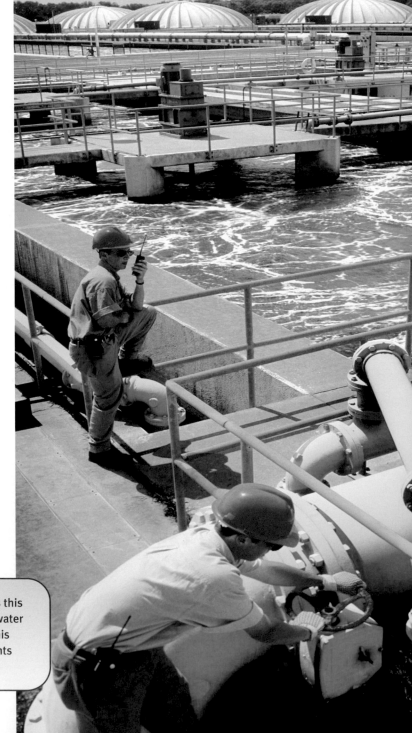

Water treatment plants, such as this one in Colorado, USA, process water so that it is safe for drinking. This processing uses up huge amounts of energy.

It is easy to take water for granted. After all, for many of us water is just something that comes out of the tap whenever we want it. In poorer parts of the world, people take very little for granted, particularly water and especially clean water. Waterborne diseases, due to unclean and untreated water, are still major killers in many parts of the world. Cholera alone affects 5.5 million people, causing 120,000 deaths each year. Waterborne diseases fill half of the developing world's hospital beds.

Water water everywhere?

The table and pie chart below show the daily and yearly water consumption in a typical home in the developed world – per person. For comparison, people in developed countries use about ten times as much water as those in poor countries, while two-fifths of the world's population face serious water shortages.

Water use	Daily amount (litres)	Annual amount (litres)
Kitchen	24	8760
Washing clothes	32	11,680
Dishwasher	1.6	584
Toilet flushing	49.6	18,104
Garden	6.4	2336
Bath	24	8760
Shower	8	2920
Personal washing (in addition to baths and showers)	14.4	4256
Total	160	58,400

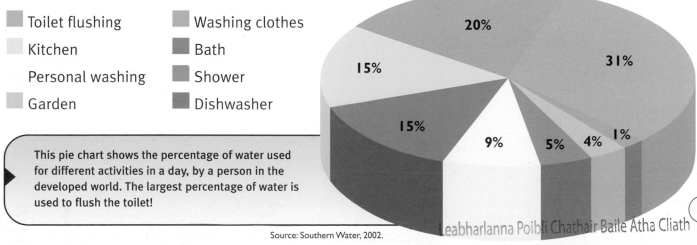

Toilet flushing · Washing clothes
Kitchen · Bath
Personal washing · Shower
Garden · Dishwasher

20% 31% 15% 15% 9% 5% 4% 1%

This pie chart shows the percentage of water used for different activities in a day, by a person in the developed world. The largest percentage of water is used to flush the toilet!

Source: Southern Water, 2002.

Flushing water away

People in developed countries use most water to flush the toilet. In the UK, homes built before about 1990 (where the toilet has not been replaced) use 9 litres of water with every flush. More modern, dual-flush toilets have two options: a long and a short flush. In addition, low-flush models or placing 'space wasters' in the cistern, which take up some of the space normally occupied by water, can help reduce water use by up to 20 per cent.

Washing water away

The average bath uses about 90 litres of water. Shorter or shallower bathtubs can be a form of passive water saving. Obviously, though, not filling the bathtub with water is a simple alternative! Showering on average uses less than half as much water as a bath, and water-efficient showerheads reduce the amount of water still more. Devices called aerators can be fitted to taps in sinks to reduce their flow without making them less efficient. Spray taps also cut down water use, but in hard-water areas, they tend to get blocked with scale and have to be treated regularly.

Having a shower instead of a bath saves water and energy. If you have an energy-efficient showerhead you can save even more water.

Case Study: Two views of saving water

Watton Green is a development of eleven houses in Birmingham, UK. The installation of 6-litre toilets, aerated taps, shallow baths and a garden water butt helped reduce water use to around 100 litres per person per day.

Look at the chart on page 21. How much of a saving on average does this represent? Can you think of additional ways to reduce this amount still further?

Before the water industry was privatised in South Africa many poor families were denied access to adequate water supplies. Now, families receive 6000 litres of water a month free. Above this amount, they pay. This means 50 litres a day for a family of 4 people. The United Nations recommends that 50 litres a day is the basic domestic water requirement. Of course, not every South African family has only four members. Does this sound like a fair system?

Water for crops

In poor or dry countries up to 80 per cent of water goes on irrigating crops. In many Indian villages, drinking water supplies from traditional wells and boreholes have been badly affected by over-extraction of groundwater for crops. Methods such as drip irrigation, which uses perforated pipes to water plants precisely, reduce waste, as do low-pressure sprinklers. Building small wall dams slows down the rate of run-off of rainfall and allows it more time to soak into the groundwater. This replenishes drinking water sources for small communities in rural areas.

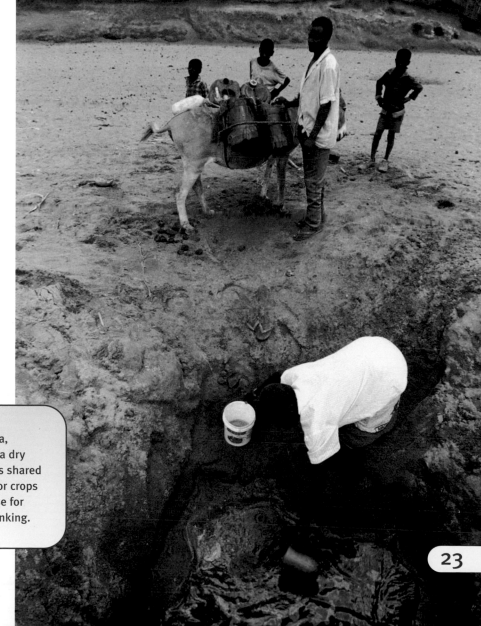

In the dusty farming district of Makueni, Kenya, families draw drinking water from this well in a dry riverbed. The small water supply in this area is shared between domestic use and farming. In order for crops to survive, farmers must pump the water to use for irrigation – meaning there is less water for drinking.

Too clean?

Treating waste water is expensive and uses large amounts of energy. The water most of us get from our taps is purified to a very high level to make it suitable for drinking. There are systems that recycle water used for washing up or showering and then treat it to a lower standard than drinking water. The recycled water is then made available again for 'non-personal' use such as flushing the toilet or gardening. This kind of system is known as a grey-water system. It saves energy and water, but is easier to install in residential accommodation such as flats rather than individual houses. Not everyone likes the idea, though, because they think it is 'dirty' water. The water isn't really dirty, but it may contain higher levels of certain chemicals depending, for example, on what cleaning products have been used. It is not suitable for drinking, but is fine for flushing the toilet!

Bringing in the rain

Of course, recycling or collecting water is nothing new. Most of us are familiar with the idea of an outside water butt that collects rainwater from the roof. Washing up water can also be emptied on to plants rather than straight down the plughole. In many countries, where water is permanently in short supply or contaminated by contact with human or animal waste, collecting rainwater is vital to survival.

Water shortage is not just a problem in hot countries in the developing world. In the developed world, too, we need to think about recycling water in our homes and gardens wherever possible.

In much of the world, particularly Asia and Africa, the collection and storage of rainwater still serves as a major source of drinking water in rural areas. Reasonably pure rainwater can be collected from roofs constructed with galvanised corrugated iron, aluminium or cement sheets, tiles, slates and even thatch. It is important to keep the roofs clean and free from bird droppings, and to have good quality storage vessels. Simple filters, such as fine cotton cloth, can also be used to remove any particles of dirt.

Case study: Water crisis in the Lebanon

In the Lebanon, natural water scarcity, increased demand and poor waste water treatment are leading to a water crisis. Often waste water is released untreated or captured in septic tanks, which may leak, causing contamination of groundwater. Several towns in West Bekaa are testing a grey-water system for recycling the waste water using what are known as trickle filters. The aim is to use the recycled water for urban horticulture, increasing the availability of fresh food and generating income, while safeguarding freshwater supplies. High levels of community involvement are important if the idea is to be successful and introduced more widely in the country.

This rainwater collection system in Belize catches water that falls on the roofs of nearby huts in a tank. The water has not been contaminated by contact with human or animal waste and is reasonably pure as long as the roofs are kept clean.

Treating waste water

In most developed countries, modern waste water treatment works are very efficient, but the treatment is expensive and also uses a lot of water. There are more sustainable ways of treating our own waste, depending on location, although they will not always be appropriate or even possible.

Reed bed system

Reed beds are natural water purifiers. Certain kinds of reed have the ability to absorb oxygen from the air and release it through their roots. This creates ideal conditions for the development of huge numbers of micro-organisms that are able to break down human or other waste.

Treating waste water

In a typical reed bed system sewage and other waste water is collected in underground tanks. The liquid is pumped into a 'filtering stack' where it trickles down through stone chippings before entering a planted reed bed. This is a large tank of reeds planted on graded gravel, topped with sand. From here, the treated liquid enters a lake via a marshy area. By now it is free of any harmful organisms such as bacteria. The remaining solids settle for a while and are then pumped out to a 'sludge bed', which is planted with another kind of reed. The solids are allowed to form compost and are then dug out every ten years for use as fertiliser.

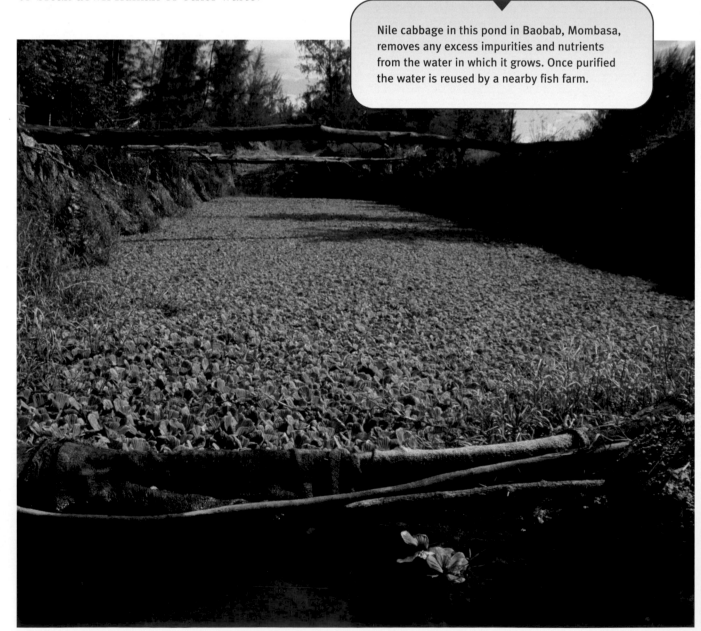

Nile cabbage in this pond in Baobab, Mombasa, removes any excess impurities and nutrients from the water in which it grows. Once purified the water is reused by a nearby fish farm.

A big PR problem?

Perhaps for obvious reasons, dry toilets are not popular. In Mexico, modern (water-based) sanitation is undermining the stability of the soil as more and more groundwater is pumped out to meet demand. A flushing toilet is a status symbol, since it is a visible sign of wealth. Education and pointing out the advantages of dry systems, which include lower costs, takes time and is not always successful. How would you 'sell' the idea of dry toilets to a doubtful family? How would you feel about having one installed in your home?

Dry toilets can dispose of sewage just as effectively as flush toilets, but without wasting valuable water.

A reed bed system must suit the circumstances and landscape of a particular site and not all designs are the same. In India, lilies are grown in the water, rather than reeds. In parts of South America, Asia and Africa, waste stabilisation ponds are widely used. These are shallow lakes where treatment of waste water occurs through the natural biological activities of algae and bacteria.

Dry toilets

Dry or composting toilets go one step further. They don't use water at all. Basically they consist of two vaults: one in use, and the other composting. In the vault that is in use the waste material is constantly covered with lime or ash. These dry toilets can be installed inside or outside the house and are inexpensive to build. Designed properly they don't smell, and the waste is a valuable source of fertiliser.

A good compromise?

In parts of rural India and China, a compromise solution to the dry toilet is a 'pour-flush' twin-pit toilet, which uses the minimum amount of water to clean the small toilet pan. This water is usually household waste water. This kind of toilet is more popular than a dry toilet and also saves the ash or lime, which can then be used to improve soil instead. As with this example, living in a sustainable home may sometimes mean striking a balance between an ideal solution and a practical one.

CHAPTER 4

Reducing waste and cutting pollution

On average, a person living in Europe produces about half a ton of household waste or rubbish each year. In the USA the average is three-quarters of a ton per person. In order to make our homes more sustainable we must reduce the amount of unnecessary waste we produce.

In both Europe and the USA about half of waste ends up in landfill sites and many regions are now running out of places to bury it. Landfill generates methane, which is a powerful greenhouse gas, as the rubbish decomposes. Although this is sometimes piped off for use as a fuel, in the form of biogas, most of it escapes. In Europe a further 17 per cent (14 per cent in the USA) of waste is burned in incinerators. This can also be a valuable source of energy, but few people want waste incinerators near their homes.

Reduce: use less: gain more

Since over 25 per cent of dustbin waste is packaging, avoiding over-packaged goods is a good way to reduce waste. Removing your house address from mailing lists, using 'mail preference services', can reduce the amount of junk mail and free newspaper drops you receive. This can be quite complicated, however, and different countries operate different systems. In the USA, 5.6 million tons of junk mail is sent out every year and 44 per cent of it is never even opened.

> Burning rubbish in incinerators is one way of dealing with rubbish, but it would be far better for the environment if we produced less rubbish in the first place. The emissions from this chimney are contributing to global warming and may contain toxic products.

28

Taking part in recycling schemes can contribute to a sustainable lifestyle and is just one of the things that you can do to reduce the amount of waste that ends up in landfills. Recycling saves energy, resources and land.

Reuse again and again

Reusing items such as carrier bags and using waste paper for scrap are obvious examples of ways we can reuse items. Charity shops are also brilliant at recycling goods. In poorer countries very few items are ever thrown away because they are seen as valuable resources that can be used for other purposes. Oil cans become sheet metal statues or model cars, and plastic containers become water carriers.

Here is a small challenge – before throwing something away think if there is another use for it, or before buying a new item check if there is something already in your home that you could use instead.

Recycle: don't just throw it away

All developed countries have some system of local government or authority that provides local services such as refuse (rubbish) collection, recreational facilities or social services. Most of these authorities also run recycling schemes. Often they are doorstep or kerbside collections for items such as paper, plastic, glass, aluminium and steel cans. The USA, which recycles 32 per cent of its domestic waste, now has over 9000 kerbside collections as well as 12,000 'drop-off' centres for recyclable material. Some authorities provide additional recycling facilities for textiles and garden waste, which could also be composted at home.

"If you do your recycling of your newspapers, you're saving on the cutting down of trees – recycling stops rubbish being dumped on the countryside."

Pensioner

"Actually, I can't see the point [of recycling]; I don't produce enough rubbish to make a difference and, anyway, the time needed to sort it is just not worth the trouble."

Person moving into flats run in a sustainable way

Recycling in developing countries

In many rapidly developing countries recycling takes place by individuals as a matter of necessity, and sometimes survival. Large urban rubbish tips, in countries such as Brazil, support whole communities that scavenge for reusable or recyclable materials, often at great risk to themselves. This does not mean organised recycling does not happen. Many South American countries, including Brazil, Argentina and Uruguay, have passed what are known as Extended Producer Responsibility (EPR) laws. This means that manufacturers of certain products, such as batteries, lamps and printer cartridges, have to provide facilities to take them back once they are used, so they can be recycled or disposed of safely.

Recycling in the developed world

Most householders are willing to go to a bit of extra trouble to separate out their waste, but in many countries more encouragement and better recycling facilities could increase recycling rates dramatically. In Switzerland it is an offence not to separate out waste. In Germany, people are charged by how much they throw away. Look at the recycling records for Switzerland and Germany in the bar chart (below). Do you think the laws about recycling in these countries are a good idea, or should people be allowed to make up their own minds?

The "Castle", in New Mexico, USA, is a home made of beer cans and mud. It is the first of several sustainable buildings designed to show what can be achieved using waste materials and sustainable methods.

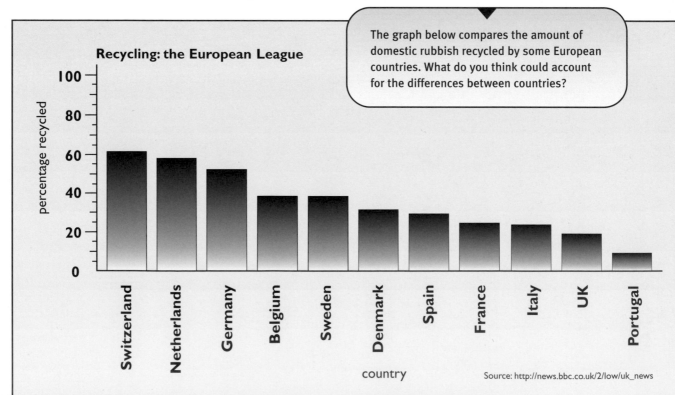

Recycling: the European League

The graph below compares the amount of domestic rubbish recycled by some European countries. What do you think could account for the differences between countries?

percentage recycled

100
80
60
40
20
0

Switzerland — Netherlands — Germany — Belgium — Sweden — Denmark — Spain — France — Italy — UK — Portugal

country

Source: http://news.bbc.co.uk/2/low/uk_news

Using less harmful materials

As well as generating waste, our homes can also be a source of harmful or toxic substances. Some of these may be responsible for the large increases in asthma and other allergic reactions experienced by people in many parts of the world. Some substances may even cause cancer. Others can cause direct damage to the environment and to wildlife.

In countries that can obtain wood grown from sustainable resources, timber window frames are preferable to frames made from uPVC, which is a type of plastic. The manufacture of uPVC involves the use of oil (itself, a non-renewable resource) and also releases toxic chemicals called dioxins. Natural paints, varnishes and some types of glue give off fewer harmful fumes than oil-based products. Insulation can be made out of cellulose (obtained from wood or recycled paper) rather than materials made from oil or minerals.

Homes made with timber frames are environmentally friendly as long as the timber comes from a sustainably managed forest where new trees are planted as mature trees are cut down.

Hurting the poor

In countries where wood is scarce, harmful building materials are frequently used because they are cheap. Asbestos sheeting is sometimes dumped on poorer countries by richer nations, where its use is now banned because dust from asbestos is highly carcinogenic or cancer inducing. A far better alternative is ferro-cement, which uses a minimum of cement mix, reinforced with wire mesh, to produce a lightweight, cost-effective building material. Roof sections, beams and posts, doors, window frames, rafters and composting toilets can be made using this technology. In India, ferro-cement is also used widely for constructing tanks for collecting rainwater.

Killer in the cupboard?

Bleach-based cleaning products and disinfectants, designed to kill germs, can harm the micro-organisms that break down waste material in water treatment works. Perhaps more worrying are the many new and complex chemicals found in products such as stain removers, flame retardants, food packaging, floor polishes, household lubricants, food packaging and even children's toys (see page 33).

We can't always avoid using products like these in the home, but we can be more aware of the possible dangers they pose. In Europe products meeting high environmental standards have a distinctive eco-label. Plastics with the number 3 or 7 inside the recycling logo are likely to contain harmful substances called phthalates. In the USA, of the 87,000 chemicals on the market only a

tiny percentage have been tested for long-term toxic effects. Although the US Food and Drugs Administration requires comprehensive labelling of products it is easy to hide potentially toxic chemicals under trade or other names.

The issue of household chemicals is complex because not all of the scientific research is completely proven. In the end, it is probably sensible to be sparing when using any manufactured household product and to try and use more natural or organic alternatives whenever possible.

Many of the cleaning products we are familiar with in our homes are more dangerous than we think.

Chemicals on the danger list

Many chemicals found in modern products remain in the environment for a long time. They can build up in our bodies and in those of wild animals. This is especially true in the case of top predators, such as seals or birds of prey. The chemicals pass up, and become more concentrated, in the food chain. Substances called phthalates, used as plastic softeners, are known as hormone disrupters. They block the normal action of hormones, especially sex hormones. This may lead to conditions such as testicular cancer. Other chemicals called phenols, used in computer cases, crash helmets and the plastic lining of food cans, have been shown to have a 'feminising' effect on molluscs, fish and birds, although their effects on humans are not known.

Common seals such as this one are at great risk from pollution caused by chemicals from household waste. Since they are top predators, toxic chemicals build up in the food chain and become concentrated in animals such as this.

33

Positive action

As well as thinking about the negative impact of our homes on the environment, we also need to look at the idea of sustainable homes as having a positive effect. Good designs that fit in with the local surroundings will enhance the environment. Using local materials and skills, and so creating local jobs, also has a positive effect. Buying locally grown food for the home cuts down on transport bills and fuel as well as supporting local farmers. For those with gardens or allotments, growing vegetables also makes homes more sustainable. At the same time, waste plant material can be used to make compost, which reduces the need for artificial fertilisers.

Growing organic food

Organically grown food has had no chemical fertilisers or pesticides used on it at all. There is general agreement that this is better for the environment because pesticides kill beneficial organisms as well as ones that damage crops. Organic food may also be better for our health. It is, however, more expensive than conventionally grown products. The benefits to the environment may well be worth this additional cost. These benefits include stopping the long-term damage done to soil structure by the continuous use of chemical fertilisers.

Growing your own vegetables can make your home more sustainable. It is important to make sure, however, that the soil has not been contaminated by past industrial use.

A crew of foresters in Costa Rica plant trees in the Puriscal region for the environmental group Arbofilia. This project brings farmers and nursery workers together to reforest the land and manage it sustainably

It is also important to think about organic produce when buying food from overseas, particularly from developing countries. Unless the food is organically grown, poor farmers are often exposed to high levels of toxic chemicals with little protection or knowledge of the health risks they face. Buying food from poorer countries with some kind of 'fair trade' labelling also means that the original growers have received a reasonable price for their produce and are not being exploited. This in turn reduces poverty. This is important in itself, but more so because poor people are often forced to damage their environment in order to obtain the resources they need. Reducing poverty can also benefit the environment by preventing the need for this damage.

Better buildings

The building materials we use can also have a positive effect. Timber frame construction using timber grown from a sustainable source means that mature trees, which have finished growing and are carbon neutral, are replaced by saplings, which are growing rapidly and therefore absorb more carbon dioxide. Labelling of sustainably-grown timber is now covered by various internationally recognised schemes – principally the Forestry Stewardship Council (FSC) scheme and the Pan European Forest Certification Scheme.

Timber is an excellent building material that keeps buildings cool in the summer and reduces heating costs in the winter. The use of toxic glues can be reduced by using the wood's natural lignin, instead. In one construction system, pre-formed timber panels are built with cellulose fibre insulation already sandwiched between the panels. This reduces waste and means the panels have what is known as low embodied energy. This means that as little energy as possible goes into their construction and transport.

Providing food for birds is just one way of supporting your local wildlife and making your home more sustainable. Make sure the food is fresh and any nuts are unsalted. Birds in the garden are also beneficial because they help to control insect pests. If you start feeding birds in your garden, remember that you must feed them all year round – not just in the winter.

Learning to live with wildlife

We tend to think of human habitation as being damaging to wildlife or the habitats where wild animals and plants live, and often it is. But in most homes there is likely to be some kind of open space near by, whether it is in the form of a garden, yard, green space, communal area or just a window box. The way this space is managed, for example the type of plants grown there, can greatly benefit local wildlife. Similarly the avoidance of garden chemicals, such as slug killers or pesticides (for which there are many natural alternatives) will also have a positive impact on wildlife. In fact, killing garden pests can often do more harm than good because beneficial species may also be eliminated.

Supporting your local wildlife

You can support your local wildlife by:

- providing food for birds, such as nuts (not salted), fat and sunflower seeds

- putting out water for birds to drink and possibly bathe in
- putting up nest boxes; keeping them out of direct sunlight and out of reach of predators
- adding compost or rotting leaves to soil to make it richer and to improve the habitat for small insects (and to benefit the larger animals, such as hedgehogs, frogs and birds, that feed on them)
- sprinkling wildflower seeds in a suitable corner; once grown, these will attract butterflies and other insects
- if space allows, building a small pond to benefit frogs and dragonflies; add a small plank or large stones so animals can get out
- creating dark, damp corners for amphibians such as frogs, toads and newts
- planting 'cover' such as hedges or shrubs; this will encourage insects and songbirds.

Location, location

Ideally, new sustainable homes should be built on what are called brownfield sites. These are sites on which previous housing or industrial premises have existed. This is not always possible, or even desirable. In some cases, industrial land is polluted with toxic chemicals such as lead and cadmium.

Removing polluted soil is costly and can expose workers to health hazards. When greenfield sites – sites that have not previously been built on – are chosen, care needs to be taken to avoid land that is ecologically important. However, brownfield sites may also develop interesting or rare wildlife over time and these, too, need to be protected.

Case Study: Building homes for people and nature

Loudoun County eco-village is situated in 0.72 square kilometres of organically managed land in Northern Virginia, USA. The village follows the natural contours of the land and biodiversity (the variety of living things) is maintained by careful land planning and planting. Construction practices preserve existing forest, soil and water. Landscaping is based on native plants, ground cover and wildflowers. Cars are excluded from the centre of the village and there are many pedestrian trails allowing residents to move around the village and enjoy its natural features.

"Living here has given me a feeling of connection to nature and our neighbours; I have found a neighbourhood that reflects my values."

Resident

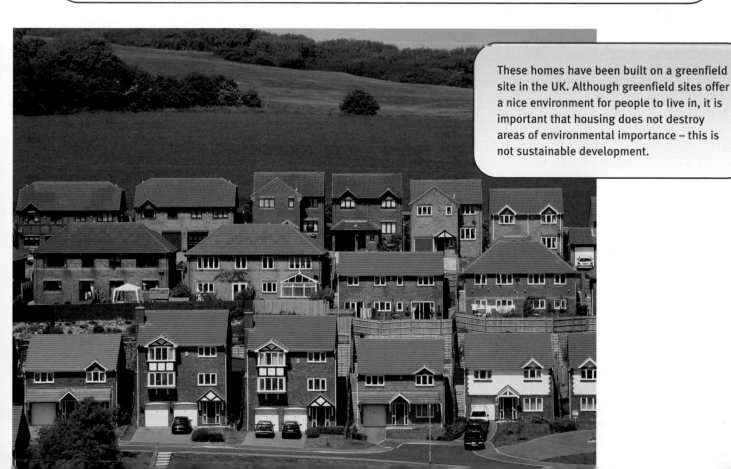

These homes have been built on a greenfield site in the UK. Although greenfield sites offer a nice environment for people to live in, it is important that housing does not destroy areas of environmental importance – this is not sustainable development.

Building sustainable communities

Perhaps the most important factor that makes a home a good place to live, is the community: the people who live there. But what do we really mean by sustainable communities? They are places where people work together to create a fairer, more sustainable way of doing things. Rather than working individually they share resources and ideas to produce a better quality of life for everyone.

Better homes for people

In most countries, both rich and poor, many people find it hard to find good quality, affordable housing in the places they want to live and work. Sustainable communities are attempts to combine these ideas in a way that does not make unsustainable demands on resources. Often they are partnerships between local authorities, local businesses and voluntary organisations that share the same vision of a more sustainable future.

"Creating sustainable communities means putting sustainable development into practice. Sustainable communities must combine social inclusion [involving people], homes, jobs, services, infrastructure [local services and transport] and respect for the environment, to create places where people will want to live and work now and in the future."

John Prescott, UK Deputy Prime Minister

Carefully planned and well-designed housing can provide people with a better quality of life. In previously run-down areas, new developments like this one have shown an improvement in people's well-being and have encouraged residents to take better care of their homes and the environment.

Communities such as this one in San Jose, California, USA, share common ideas about the environment they want to live in. This can lead to less vandalism and people looking after their surroundings by not dropping litter for example.

This is not just a question of reducing energy use or cutting down waste. It is about building communities that work better in a more general sense. They are sometimes described as being 'socially inclusive'. This means that everyone, whatever their beliefs, ethnic origin or background, feels part of a community where different views are tolerated and valued, and responsibilities shared. The homes themselves should be well designed and well built and, as far as possible, fit in with the local environment. They should have good transport services and other forms of communication linking people to jobs, schools, health services, leisure facilities, shops and other services. They should also be fair: everyone, no matter what their situation, should benefit equally from the services and resources available. Finally, of course, they should be environmentally sensitive: providing places for people to live that take account of the needs of the environment.

Communities working together and sharing common ideas and goals tend to work better than those that do not. There are often other benefits, too, such as lower crime rates, less vandalism, better individual health and more 'social interaction'. In short, people have more say in what goes on in their community, and therefore value it more highly.

Getting the infrastructure right

Sustainable communities are not about building sustainable homes in isolation. Of equal importance are the many services, such as shops and other facilities needed to support that community – the infrastructure. Unless the right services are available, in the right places, and within reach of the people who need them, many of the benefits of sustainable housing will be lost.

Transport and communication

Transport and communication are crucial when developing sustainable communities. Look at the example in the box (right). Make a list of the different services and other features mentioned, and their distance from the community. How do you think these features contribute to making this community more sustainable? Many of the developments are designed to reduce car use. This will reduce the overall energy consumption of the community and cut down pollution. To achieve this the provision of

efficient and affordable public transport, such as trains, buses and trams, within easy reach of the community is essential.

A question of communications

A housing group in Firgrove, UK, developed a small group of two-bedroom houses in a built-up area. The houses are 500 metres from a bus stop with routes to several towns and the railway station. A post box and food shop are also within 500 metres of the scheme. A post office, chemist, school, medical centre, community centre and public house are all within 1 kilometre. A footpath connects the site to the bus stop and local facilities. Space is made available in one of the bedrooms in each house for a home office. Secure cycle storage is also provided.

If everyone in a community uses public transport instead of cars for short journeys an enormous amount of fuel can be saved. This also means fewer emissions and a healthier environment. Public transport must be clean and reliable, like this modern tram in Strasbourg, if people are going to be encouraged to use it.

Case Study: L.A. eco-village

Los Angeles eco-village in the USA is only one block (a few hundred metres) east of one of L.A.'s busiest traffic corridors. It is part of a 2-block neighbourhood consisting of 48 housing units. The buildings are gradually being refurbished to reduce their environmental impact. In addition there is a demonstration grey-water system (see page 24), an electric vehicle sharing scheme and the co-operative buying of organic food and environmentally safe household products.

Perhaps just as important as these features, however, is the thinking behind the project. The idea is to demonstrate how a diverse, or mixed, population can live more sustainably in an urban environment, as one of the residents describes:

"We try to figure out how the problems in our neighbourhood are related to the problems in the wider environment. We are especially interested in how these problems relate to our ability to have healthy air, water and soil, human health, a decent standard of living, a high quality of life, non-polluting livelihood, and a strong sense of community. Through working together with our own skills and resources we begin to create changes in our neighbourhood at the pace we can incorporate them into our lives physically, socially and economically. There is much opportunity for collaboration and building consensus [agreement)]."

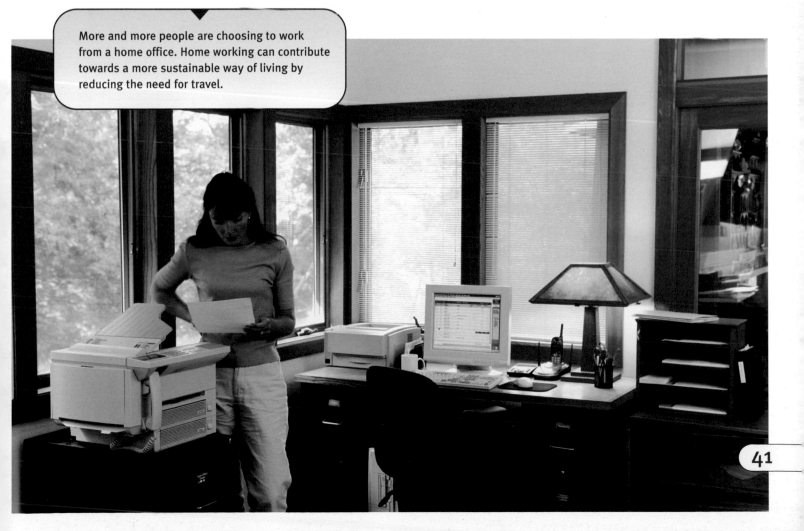

More and more people are choosing to work from a home office. Home working can contribute towards a more sustainable way of living by reducing the need for travel.

The United Nations Climate Change Conference

Former president Bill Clinton said at the 2005 United Nations Climate Change conference that cutting greenhouse gases was good for the planet. At the 2008 conference President Obama promised "a new chapter of American leadership on climate change".

Using the power of government

Most governments now recognise the connection between sustainable communities and healthy societies. They have also become concerned about the impact of human activity on the environment. In particular, the effects of global warming have forced governments and other bodies, especially those in developed countries, to bring in tough new standards for constructing homes and other buildings that are designed to reduce energy use.

In Europe the 'Energy Performance of Buildings Directive' requires all member states to set minimum standards of energy-efficiency on all new buildings, as well as on large buildings undergoing major renovation. In a typical European country the aim is to improve energy-efficiency in domestic homes by an average of 20 per cent by 2010 compared to 2000. It is calculated that energy standards of new homes will deliver a reduction in carbon emissions of 1.4 million tons a year.

Many of these regulations go far beyond the use of energy. Increasingly governments are developing standards for the efficient use of resources generally, including those relating to water, transport and waste.

"In years to come this is what we've got to use; low energy lights. That's all there is to it."

Resident living in environmental flats

"The [low energy] lights are so cheap to run you can use as much as you like. So I leave all the lights on."

Pensioner

Not for everyone?

Not everyone will share the same views about sustainable communities, or want to be involved. This is particularly true where people move into the community without understanding or being part of the vision that created the community in the first place. For example, some people prefer to use ordinary light bulbs rather than feeling they have to use low energy ones. Or, because low energy bulbs cost less to run, they feel they can use them more. Saving waste, such as paper or plastic, may also be seen in very different ways.

Other people may be prepared to act in ways that are more sustainable when it saves them money or time, but not when there is inconvenience or no saving to themselves. For example, providing good public transport systems does not necessarily mean people will use them if it is more convenient to take the car. Look at the views on this page. What do you think about these issues? People need to be convinced of the benefits before they

will participate fully, and even when the benefits are clear it takes time to build new communities.

> *"I guess it's the guilt, isn't it? You live in an environmentally friendly house, so you feel like you ought to do it [recycle]."*
>
> Resident of environmentally friendly housing

> *"In winter time you're in and out in all weathers to put a couple of bits of plastic in one bin and a bit of newspaper in another. So it doesn't really make it easy for you."*
>
> New resident to environmentally friendly housing

New houses have to be built with energy-saving and other sustainable measures in mind. Housing will only continue to become more sustainable through a mixture of government regulation and action by individuals.

No place like a sustainable home

There are many different kinds of sustainable home and many different approaches to living in a sustainable community. It may involve a purpose-built eco-village where everything is designed to minimise the impact on the environment. It may be a small group of new homes built to high environmental standards. It may be an old housing estate or city block that is gradually renovated to be more energy-efficient. It may be in a poor rural area or in a city anywhere in the world.

For each of these different approaches to sustainable living, different solutions are needed. Some of these will require governments and planners to act; others will require investment in new technologies by industry and other bodies; some will require communities themselves to take control.

This home is built into a hillside. It is extremely eco-friendly and a great example of sustainable living. The glass windows let in heat and light and this heat is retained well by the surrounding hillside.

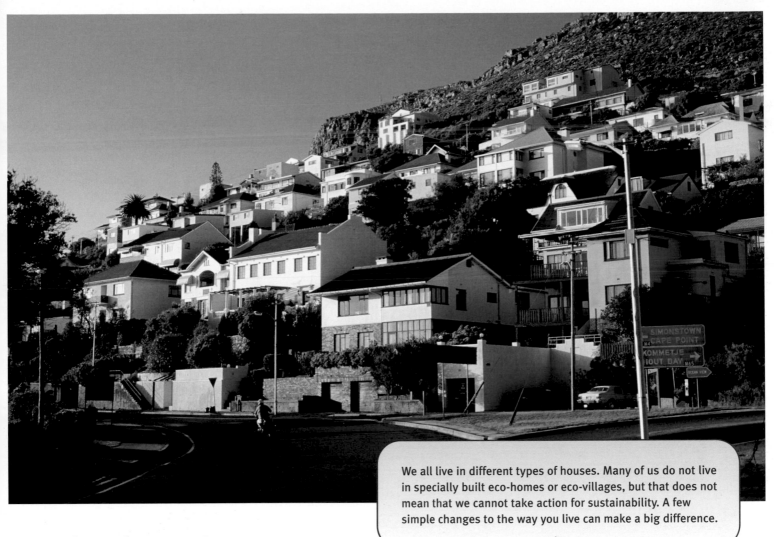

We all live in different types of houses. Many of us do not live in specially built eco-homes or eco-villages, but that does not mean that we cannot take action for sustainability. A few simple changes to the way you live can make a big difference.

What about us?

While it may be easier to plan and build new sustainable homes, the reality is that most of us will continue to live in ordinary, existing homes in ordinary towns, cities and villages. But that does not mean we can't go some way to making those homes and communities more sustainable. You could, of course, ask, "Why bother?" Most people now recognise that the majority of us – whether in rich or poor countries, and for different reasons – are living in ways that are unsustainable; that are damaging the environment and, in the process, harming ourselves as well. Unless we somehow change the way we live, the consequences may be serious for us all.

It is sometimes hard to feel you have any influence over these issues. However, change is always possible, particularly if you feel it is important enough. For example, you could look at the way you travel to school or other locations. You may have already done this.

Many schools now encourage more sustainable ways of travelling to and from the site. How could this be promoted more effectively? Youth groups and clubs are also good places to look for ways of doing things more sustainably. If you have access to the Internet, try typing in the name of your district and the words 'sustainable communities.' See what you find! The local library or council offices should also have plenty of information. Finally, you can also change what you do in your home itself.

Your choice

Living more sustainably is a matter of choice. After all, why should you change the way you live if others are not prepared to do the same? Sustainable homes are not just fine ideas for those who can afford them; they are at the heart of successful and healthy communities, worldwide. In the end, it is your community and your choice.

45

Glossary

asbestos highly heat-resistant substance used in fire-resistant and insulating materials. Asbestos particles can cause cancer if inhaled.

biogas name given to the mix of gases produced by rotting organic matter

biomass organic matter used as a fuel. Biomass is often used to generate electricity.

borehole deep narrow hole in the ground that is drilled to find water

carcinogenic substance that can cause cancer

CHP (combined heat and power) efficient technology in which the heat produced during the generation of electricity is recovered and used

deforestation clearing of trees from an area

developed countries wealthy countries that are technologically advanced

developing countries financially poor and technologically unsophisticated countries that are becoming more advanced

dioxin extremely toxic substance that is produced as a by-product of some manufacturing processes

ecology relation of organisms to one another and to their physical surroundings

fair trade trade that involves developing world farmers being paid a fair price for their produce

fermenter a container in which organic material is broken down by natural processes to produce either methane gas or alcohol, either of which can be used as fuels

ferro-cement strong, light building material with less cement than normal concrete

fossil fuel substance such as coal, oil and gas that is formed from the decomposition of animal and plant remains. Fossil fuels release carbon dioxide when they are burned.

greenhouse gas gas, such as carbon dioxide, that contributes to global warming and climate change

groundwater water from underground sources

incinerator place where waste can be burned

irrigation supply of water to the land, usually for growing crops

lignin substance found in the cell walls of many plants and trees

microclimate climate of a small area such as a wood or even inside a building

organic derived from living organisms

photovoltaic cells devices that are used to produce electricity using direct sunlight

PV array group of photovoltaic cells

raw material basic material from which a product is made. Oil is one of the raw materials of plastic.

refurbish repair something to bring it back into good working order. A refurbished house is one that has been made fit to live in.

resources assets or materials that are valuable. The world's natural resources include water and fossil fuels such as coal, gas and oil.

slurry runny mixture usually made up of manure, cement or coal, and water

toxic poisonous

Further information

Websites and organisations

www.bioregional.com

Website for the Beddington Zero Energy Development (BedZED), the UK's largest 'carbon neutral' eco-village: carbon neutral means that no extra carbon dioxide is produced in generating energy for the village.

www.ecovillagefindhorn.com

Website for the Findhorn Foundation, based in Scotland: the aim is to create linked 'ecovillages' around the world through the Global Ecovillage Network.

www.environment-agency.gov.uk

UK Government website for the Environment Agency: deals with all aspects of environmental improvement, including saving water (www.sepa.org.uk for Scotland).

www.est.org.uk

Website of the Energy Saving Trust: provides information on all aspects of energy saving in the home, including energy-saving products, insulation and generating your own electricity!

www.foe.co.uk

Website of Friends of the Earth: produces information and educational material on all aspects of sustainability and the environment, particularly reducing pollution and waste.

www.oneplanetliving.org/index.html

Website about One Planet Living, a global initiative based on living sustainably and run by WWF.

www.rspb.org.uk

Website of the Royal Society for the Protection of Birds: provides information on improving open spaces for wildlife and also other practical issues to do with sustainability.

www.sustainablehomes.co.uk

Organisation promoting awareness of sustainable development for housing associations.

www.wastewatch.org.uk

Website of main UK organisation providing information and publications in relation to waste reduction and recycling.

www.wwf.org.uk/chemicals

WWF-UK website concerned with chemicals and health in the home and garden.

www.wwf.org.uk/sustainablehomes

See also above: website about WWF's 'One Million Sustainable Homes' campaign.

Books

Green Files: Waste and Recycling, Steve Parker (Heinemann Library, 2004)

Pachamama: Our Earth – Our Future (Evans Brothers, 2002)

Renewable Energy, Chris Oxlade and Nigel Saunders (Raintree, 2004)

Science at the Edge: Alternative Energy Sources, Sally Morgan (Heinemann Library, 2003)

Science at the Edge: Global Warming, Sally Morgan (Heinemann Library, 2003)

Sustainable Human Development: A Young Person's Introduction, Peace Child International (Evans Brothers, 2003)

Index